The Real Story  n: From Kim K to Global Influencer!

by Boris Petrovic

Table Of Contents

Chapter 1 - Dreaming of Stardom
Chapter 2 - Acting Dreams
Chapter 3 - City Lights
Chapter 4 - Sisterly Love
Chapter 5 - The Audition Hustle
Chapter 6 - Rising Star
Chapter 7 - Rapid Rise
Chapter 8 - Unexpected Love
Chapter 9 - High Society Love
Chapter 10 - Envious Flames
Chapter 11 - Pressing Issues.
Chapter 12 - Fame's Guardian
Chapter 13 - Beyond Acting
Chapter 14 - undefned
Chapter 15 - Persistence Pays Off.
Chapter 16 - Showdown on Stage
Chapter 17 - Graceful Confrontation 2
Chapter 18 - Love's Unwavering Strength
Chapter 19 - Awards and

Accolades. *Chapter 20* - Union of Power

Chapter 21 - Championing Causes.

Chapter 22 - Humility Amidst Fame. *Chapter 23* - Everlasting Bond

Chapter 24 - Balancing Act

Chapter 25 - New Life Arrival

Chapter 26 - Betrayed Ambition *Chapter 27* - Iconic Resilience

Chapter 28 - Legendary Journey.

Chapter 29 - Grateful Refection.

Chapter 30 - Legacy of Inspiration

Chapter 1
Dreaming of Stardom

Isabella grew up in a modest household. Her parents, hardworking and dedicated to their children's happiness, did not have much in terms of luxuries. However, they instilled in their daughter a sense of limitless possibility. Isabella's eyes gleamed with a fre fueled by her fervent desire to become the brightest star in Hollywood. She was always the center of attention, the star of her school plays, and the one who effortlessly commanded the attention of a room.

Isabella's dreams of stardom never faded, even as she grew into a young woman. Her beauty was matched only by her ferce ambition. With raven locks that cascaded down her back like a waterfall, Isabella was a vision of glamour and elegance. But it was her unwavering confdence that truly set her apart. She knew she was destined for greatness, and no one could convince her otherwise.

Julia, Isabella's loyal assistant, stood by her side every step of the way. With short blonde hair framing a kind face, Julia was the perfect complement to Isabella's larger-than-life personality. While Isabella may have been the glamorous face of their partnership, Julia's diligent work behind the scenes kept them both moving forward towards greater heights of success.

As Isabella began to make a name for herself in Hollywood, she became known for her relentless determination. She refused to let anyone stand in the way of her dreams. Large-scale projects were no match for her indomitable spirit. She threw herself into every role with an intensity that left those around her breathless.

But success didn't come without its challenges. Isabella faced setbacks and disappointments along the way. There were times when it seemed like her dreams would never come to fruition. Yet through it all, she remained steadfast in her pursuit of greatness.

Isabella's journey to stardom was a curious one. It was full of twists and turns, surprises and setbacks. But through it all, she remained true to herself. She knew who she was and what she wanted, and she refused to compromise on either.

As the years went by, Isabella's star continued to rise. She became a household name, beloved by fans around the world. And through it all, Julia remained by her side, always ensuring that Isabella stayed on track toward her dreams.

In many ways, Isabella's story is a symbol of the American Dream. She came from humble beginnings, but with hard work and determination, she was able to achieve greatness. And while her success may have been large-scale, it was also deeply personal. It was the result of years of hard work and sacrifce, of countless hours spent honing her craft and perfecting her skills.

Isabella's journey is a testament to the power of ambition and perseverance. It's a reminder that anything is possible if you're willing to put in the work. And as she continues to inspire new generations of aspiring actors and actresses, her legacy will live on for years to come.

Chapter 2
Acting Dreams

As Isabella entered her teenage years, her passion for acting only grew stronger. She spent countless hours honing her skills, determined to become the best she could be. Her hard work and dedication paid off as she soon began building an impressive portfolio.

Isabella's journey was large-scale in every sense of the word. Her dreams were massive, and she was willing to do whatever it took to achieve them. She worked tirelessly day after day, always eager to improve her craft. Her drive and ambition were palpable, and those around her couldn't help but be inspired by her tenacity. Despite her youth, Isabella was acutely aware of the challenges that lay ahead. She knew that the entertainment industry was highly competitive, and success was far from guaranteed. But rather than let that discourage her, she embraced the challenge with grace and poise. She was determined to navigate the industry's pitfalls with strategic planning and unwavering determination.

Thankfully, Isabella had an ally in Julia- a meticulous and dedicated partner in her journey. Julia had been by Isabella's side since the beginning of her acting journey, and she took great pride in supporting Isabella's dreams. Together, they worked tirelessly to create a portfolio that would showcase Isabella's talents to the world.

The pacing of their efforts was well-constructed. There were highs when they secured impressive roles and lows when they faced rejection or setbacks. But through it all, Isabella remained determined and focused on her goals. Each new experience was a learning opportunity, and she took every lesson to heart.

As Isabella continued to build her portfolio, it became clear that she possessed a rare talent for the craft of acting. Her performances were captivating, leaving audiences spellbound wherever she went.

Isabella's journey is a curious one- marked by incredible ambition and perseverance. She proved that anything is possible if you're willing to put in the work- even in an industry as challenging as entertainment. And as she continues to inspire new generations of aspiring actors and actresses, her legacy will live on for years to come.

Chapter 3

City Lights

Isabella's journey to the big city was a monumental one. The buzz of the metropolis was overwhelming, the towering skyscrapers seemed to stretch towards the heavens themselves, the neon lights that illuminated every corner were almost blinding. Isabella felt a sense of trepidation grip her as she looked around, but at the same time, she couldn't help but feel an excitement that coursed through her veins. She had fnally arrived at the place where she hoped to make a name for herself.

As she walked through the busy streets, she couldn't help but notice how small she felt in this large-scale world. But Isabella possessed an unshakeable ambition that refused to be intimidated by what lay ahead. She had come prepared, with a portfolio bursting with talent and a heart full of dreams.

It wasn't long before she met Julia, her future assistant. Julia was a breath of fresh air, her warm smile and frm handshake immediately putting Isabella at ease. As they sat down to discuss their plans, Isabella couldn't help but admire Julia's sharp brown eyes and short blonde hair that bounced as she spoke.

Isabella learned quickly that the industry was incredibly competitive and challenging, but with Julia by her side, she felt like anything was possible. Julia became an integral part of her team, handling everything from scheduling meetings to managing her social media presence. Isabella trusted her completely and knew that without Julia's help, she wouldn't have made it as far as she had. The two women were an unlikely pair, but they complemented each other perfectly. Isabella's fery ambition was matched by Julia's unwavering loyalty and dedication to making her dream a reality. As Isabella began booking gigs and making a name for herself in the industry, Julia remained by her side every step of the way. Their journey was marked by curious twists and turns, but together they persevered through all obstacles that stood in their way. Isabella's rise to fame wasn't easy, but she proved that hard work and dedication could make any dream a reality.

Looking back at her journey, Isabella couldn't help but feel grateful for the incredible people she had met along the way. Julia had been her rock through it all, and without her, Isabella knew that her story would have turned out very differently. Their partnership was a testament to the power of teamwork, and Isabella knew that with Julia by her side, she could conquer anything that came her way.

As she continued to pursue her dreams and inspire new generations of aspiring actors and actresses, Isabella's legacy only grew stronger. Her journey was one of determination and grit, a true testament to what it meant to pursue one's passion with everything they had.

Chapter 4
Sisterly Love

Isabella and Julia's working relationship was one that was built on a foundation of trust, understanding, and loyalty. They complemented each other in a way that was rare to see in the cutthroat world of show business, where egos and tempers often clashed.

Together, they formed a partnership that was large-scale in every conceivable way. Whether it was managing a hectic flming schedule, negotiating multi-million dollar contracts, or simply providing emotional support during times of crisis, Isabella knew that she could always rely on Julia to have her back.

But their partnership was more than just a working relationship. Over the years, they had formed a deep bond that extended far beyond the confnes of the flm set. They were friends, confdants, and trusted advisors to each other, with a closeness that was almost familial in nature.

As they worked together day after day, year after year, Julia became more than just Isabella's assistant - she became her rock. In moments of doubt or insecurity, Julia had a way of grounding her and reminding her of who she truly was.

Isabella, for her part, recognized the profound impact that Julia had on her life and career. She knew that without Julia's support and guidance, she would never have achieved the level of success and recognition that she had today.

Their partnership was like the gears of a well-oiled machine, each part seamlessly ftting together to form a whole that was greater than the sum of its parts. They were curious about each other's lives outside of work and often spoke about their families and personal dreams. Despite the pressures and demands of their high-profle careers, they always found time for each other - whether it was grabbing lunch between takes or simply checking in to make sure the other was doing okay.

Their bond was a testament to the power of teamwork, and Isabella knew that with Julia by her side, she could conquer anything that came her way. Together, they had weathered the highs and lows of show business, navigating the choppy waters of Hollywood with grace and poise.

As she continued to pursue her dreams and inspire new generations of aspiring actors and actresses, Isabella's legacy only grew stronger. Her journey was one of determination and grit, a true testament to what it meant to pursue one's passion with everything they had.

And at the heart of it all was the unbreakable bond between Isabella and Julia - a partnership that was as enduring and timeless as the movies they starred in.

Chapter 5
The Audition Hustle

The world of acting can be a fckle mistress, one moment showering an individual with accolades and the next, casting them aside like yesterday's news. Isabella had always known this, but it didn't make it any easier to stomach. Despite her unbreakable spirit, Isabella was starting to feel the weight of constant rejection and criticism. It was as if she were standing at the base of a colossal mountain, looking up at its imposing peak with trepidation.

Julia watched as Isabella's confdence began to falter. She knew how hard her friend had worked to get to where she was, and the thought of her talent going unrecognized was unbearable. Night after night, Julia scoured the city for new opportunities, determined to fnd a way to showcase Isabella's abilities.

The days turned into weeks, and the weeks turned into months. Each time an audition passed without an offer for a role, Isabella's frustration grew. She began to wonder if she had made the right choice in pursuing acting as a career. But try as she might, she couldn't shake the feeling that acting was her destiny.

As she sat alone in her apartment one evening, staring out at the sprawling city below, Isabella felt small and insignifcant. She wondered if anyone would ever recognize her talent or if she would be forever relegated to the background.

Days turned into weeks and still no new roles presented themselves.

But just as Isabella began to lose hope completely, a glimmer of opportunity appeared on the horizon. A large-scale production was in need of a lead actress, and Julia knew that Isabella was perfect for the part.

With newfound determination, Isabella threw herself into rehearsals, working tirelessly to bring her character to life. The role was complex and demanding, but with each passing day, Isabella grew more confdent in her ability to do it justice.

On opening night, Isabella stood backstage, her heart racing with anticipation. She had poured her heart and soul into this performance, and she knew that it was her moment to shine. As the curtain rose and the lights came up, Isabella stepped out onto the stage, ready to give the performance of a lifetime.

As the play unfolded, Isabella became her character, embodying every emotion and nuance with a depth that left the audience spellbound. Her performance was a triumph, a testament to her raw talent and unwavering determination.

Julia watched from the wings, her heart bursting with pride. To see her friend fnally receive the recognition she deserved was a moment she would never forget.

And so, Isabella's journey continued. With each new role came new challenges and opportunities for growth. But through it all, she remained steadfast in her commitment to pursue her passion with everything she had.

As for Julia, she remained by Isabella's side, fercely protective of her friend and always ready to go to bat for her. Their partnership was a bond that transcended time and circumstance - a testament to the enduring power of friendship and the unbreakable spirit of those who dare to dream.

Chapter 6
Rising Star

Isabella's heart raced as the cameras started rolling for her frst lead role. She felt a mix of excitement and nerves, hoping that she could deliver a performance that lived up to the expectations of her fans. She had come a long way since her early days in the big city, where she struggled to fnd acting roles and faced rejection and criticism from casting directors. But through it all, she remained steadfast in her commitment to pursue her passion with everything she had. As she stood on the set, surrounded by a large-scale crew of directors, producers, and fellow actors, Isabella couldn't help but feel a sense of awe and wonder. This was where she belonged - in front of the camera, bringing characters to life and captivating audiences with her talent and charisma.

Julia watched from the sidelines, beaming with pride as she saw her dear friend fnally achieving her dreams. Their bond had grown stronger over the years, with Julia providing unwavering support and guidance through every step of Isabella's journey. Her hair was cut in a sleek bob that highlighted her sharp cheekbones, and her warm brown eyes conveyed the unwavering loyalty and admiration she had for Isabella.

As the director called out "Action!", Isabella took a deep breath and stepped into character. She embodied the role with ease, bringing a depth of emotion and nuance that left everyone on set in awe. Her signature black hair was styled in loose waves that framed her face, which was adorned with subtle makeup that accentuated her piercing green eyes.

It was as if Isabella was born to play this role - to inhabit this character's world and bring it to life on screen. And as the scenes unfolded and the story unfolded before her eyes, Isabella knew that this was just the beginning. She had worked hard to get here, taking small roles and working her way up, until she fnally landed the lead role in a popular television show.

But she knew that there was still so much more to come. This was just one step on a long and winding path - a journey that would take her to places she had never imagined. And with Julia by her side, she was ready to face whatever lay ahead.

And so, as the cameras stopped rolling and the set cleared out for the night, Isabella took a moment to refect on how far she had come. She had faced rejection and criticism, but she had also found love and support in unexpected places. She had dared to dream big, and now, as she looked out at the world before her, she knew that anything was possible.

For Isabella, this was more than just a role - it was a symbol of everything she had worked for and everything she hoped to achieve. And with each passing day, she was one step closer to making those dreams a reality.

Chapter 7
Rapid Rise

Isabella had always believed in the power of dreams. She had once dared to dream big, and now, as she looked out at the world before her, she knew that anything was possible. Her success had been hard-won, built on a foundation of rejection and criticism from casting directors. But she had persevered, taking small roles and working her way up until fnally, she had landed the lead in a popular television show. And then, suddenly, everything changed. Isabella's fame skyrocketed; she became a household name almost overnight. Her enigmatic personality and piercing green eyes drew people in, while her confdent and elegant demeanor set her apart from others in her feld. Everywhere she went, she was met with adoration and awe. She was the embodiment of glamour and success, a symbol of hope for anyone who had ever dared to dream.

It was a strange and heady time for Isabella. She reveled in the attention of her fans, always seeking new ways to captivate audiences. And yet there was a sense of unease that lingered just beneath the surface. She knew that fame could be fckle, that one misstep could send everything crashing down around her. She needed to maintain her position at the top of the ladder, to keep climbing higher and higher until she reached the very pinnacle of success.

Thankfully, Julia was there to help her navigate this new world. Her short blonde hair framed her gentle face, and her brown eyes sparkled with pride as she watched Isabella's rise to stardom. She remained efcient and discreet, always looking out for Isabella's best interests and ensuring that nothing tarnished her reputation.

Together they navigated the strange world of show business, with all its glitz and glamour but also its cutthroat competition and backstabbing politics. Isabella learned quickly how to play the game, how to keep herself in the headlines without ever revealing too much of herself. Her life became a carefully curated performance, with every move calculated to maintain her position as the biggest star in the business.

And yet, even as her fame grew, there was a part of Isabella that remained curious about the world beyond the spotlight. She longed for something more than just the trappings of success - something deeper and more meaningful. She began to explore new interests, taking up painting and exploring the outdoors whenever she had a spare moment. It was during one of these excursions that Isabella stumbled upon something truly remarkable. She was hiking in a remote wilderness area when she came across a massive boulder, its surface covered in intricate carvings. As she looked closer, she realized that the carvings were actually a map, charting out the path to a hidden cave deep in the heart of the mountains.

Isabella felt a thrill of excitement run through her. This was exactly what she had been searching for - something large-scale and mysterious, something that would challenge her in new ways and push her beyond the confnes of her carefully curated life. She set out at once, determined to fnd the cave and uncover its secrets. The journey was arduous, but Isabella never faltered. She climbed steep cliffs and crossed treacherous ravines, driven by an unshakeable sense of purpose. And fnally, after days of grueling travel, she found herself standing before the cave entrance.

There was something eerie and otherworldly about the place. The air was thick with an almost palpable energy, like something was waiting just beyond reach. Isabella steeled herself and stepped inside.

What she found there was beyond anything she could have imagined. The cave was flled with ancient artifacts and strange symbols, each one more mysterious than the last. There were tablets carved with inscrutable writing, maps that seemed to show routes through impossible landscapes, and strange machines that hummed with an otherworldly energy.

Isabella explored the cave for hours, her mind buzzing with possibilities. She felt like she had stumbled upon a secret world, one that few others had ever glimpsed. And yet, even as she marveled at the wonders before her, there was a nagging sense of unease. She realized then that this was only the beginning of her journey - that there was still so much more to discover. The world was vast and full of mysteries, and Isabella knew that she had only scratched the surface. But for the frst time in a long while, she felt truly alive - driven by a sense of curiosity and wonder that had been missing from her carefully curated life.

As she emerged from the cave, Isabella knew that nothing would ever be the same again. Her fame and success were still important to her, but they were no longer the only things that mattered. She had found something larger than herself, something that would drive her forward no matter where her journey took her next. And with each passing day, she was one step closer to making those dreams a reality.

Chapter 8
Unexpected Love

Isabella had reached the peak of her career. She was a star, adored by millions and with a schedule to match. Her life seemed large-scale and impressive, but it was not without its drawbacks. Despite her growing fame and success, she felt lonely, disconnected from those around her and unsure of how to balance her personal life with her public persona. It was during this time that Isabella met Marcus, a wealthy businessman who would become her love interest. With his arrival came a newfound sense of excitement and possibility in Isabella's life. Marcus was drawn to Isabella's confdence and poise, while Isabella found solace in his warmth and companionship.

But their relationship was not without its challenges. As a businessman, Marcus was used to being in control and making calculated decisions; yet Isabella's magnetic presence had thrown him off balance. Together, they began to navigate the complexities of their shared worlds, wondering if they could fnd happiness amidst the pressures of fame and fortune.

As Isabella and Marcus grew closer, their lives began to intersect more frequently. They attended high-profle events together, traveled the world, and enjoyed each other's company in private moments. The paparazzi followed them relentlessly, capturing every moment of their relationship for the world to see. It seemed as though nothing could tear them apart.

But even in the midst of their happiness, Isabella could not help but wonder if their relationship was sustainable. She had built her career on her own terms, working tirelessly to achieve success through sheer determination and hard work. Could she really trust someone else to be there for her, no matter what the future held?

Marcus, for his part, was equally uncertain. He had never been one for grand gestures or emotional displays; yet he found himself drawn to Isabella's vulnerability and warmth in ways he could not explain. As he watched her navigate the world of celebrity with grace and poise, he felt a deep sense of admiration and respect for her. But he also knew that their relationship would require sacrifce and compromise on both sides.

As the days turned into weeks, and the weeks into months, Isabella and Marcus continued to grapple with these questions. They traveled the world together, exploring new places and experiencing new things.

They laughed and loved and learned from each other, cherishing every moment they had together.

And then, unexpectedly, everything changed. Isabella received an offer for a role that would take her away from Marcus for months on end. It was a once-in-a-lifetime opportunity, but it would mean sacrifcing the time they had built together. Could their relationship survive such a test?

In the end, Isabella decided to take the role. She had always been ambitious, driven by a ferce desire to succeed. But as she boarded the plane for her new adventure, she knew that Marcus would be waiting for her when she returned. Their relationship might face challenges in the future, but with each passing day, they grew stronger and more committed to each other.

As for Marcus, he watched Isabella go with a mixture of pride and sadness. He knew that she was destined for great things; it was one of the things he admired most about her. But he also knew that their relationship was worth fghting for. As he hugged her goodbye at the airport, he whispered in her ear:

"Go out there and conquer the world, my love. I'll be waiting for you when you get back."

Chapter 9
High Society Love

Isabella and Marcus were living a life that seemed to be plucked straight out of a fairytale. Their love was large-scale, as was their success. The couple was constantly attending glamorous events, rubbing elbows with A-list celebrities, and living in the lap of luxury. Isabella's emerald green dress fowed elegantly behind her as she strolled arm-in-arm with Marcus down the red carpet. The color of her dress seemed to symbolize her growth - from the small roles she once took to the lead role she now commanded. Her piercing green eyes shone with a mixture of happiness and excitement, and it was clear that she was living her dream.

Marcus, too, looked dashing in his tailored black tuxedo. His deep brown eyes shone with adoration for Isabella, and he couldn't help but feel lucky to be by her side. The couple was positively giddy as they made their way through the crowds of fans and paparazzi. As they entered the exclusive party, champagne fowed and laughter flled the air. The room was flled with A-list celebrities, all mingling and enjoying the company of one another. For a moment, Isabella and Marcus felt invincible. They had worked hard to get to where they were, and now they were reaping the rewards. The pacing of their lives mirrored their success - it was fast-paced and exciting. They were constantly moving, constantly attending events, constantly being photographed. But despite all the glitz and glamour, they remained grounded in their love for one another.

Their love was curious in a way - it seemed almost too good to be true. But it was real, and they both knew it. As they danced the night away, surrounded by opulence and extravagance, they felt grateful for all that they had achieved.

Their relationship was worth fghting for - that much was clear. And as Marcus hugged Isabella goodbye at the airport, he whispered in her ear, "Go out there and conquer the world, my love. I'll be waiting for you when you get back."

And conquer the world she did. Isabella continued to rise to new heights in her career, and with Marcus by her side, there was no limit to what they could achieve. Their love story was one that would go down in history - a tale of two people who started from humble beginnings and soared to unimaginable heights.

Chapter 10
Envious Flames

The Hollywood event was in full swing, with the elite of the industry mingling and laughing as they sipped their cocktails. Isabella, the enchanting actress who had captured the hearts of millions, was radiant as she made her way through the crowd. Her long black hair fowed over her shoulder, and her piercing green eyes shone like jewels in the light. She exuded confdence and elegance, a true star in every sense of the word.

Little did Isabella know that Victoria, her rival actress, was also at the event. With her long red hair pulled back into a tight bun and icy blue eyes scanning the room, Victoria was seething with jealousy as she watched Isabella mingling with the elite of Hollywood. She knew that Isabella's success had come at her expense, and she was determined to bring her down.

As Isabella laughed and took pictures with other celebrities, Victoria began hatching her next plan to ruin the successful actress. She knew that she needed to strike Isabella where it hurt the most, and so she began to plot a large-scale attack on her rival's career. Over the next few weeks, Victoria worked tirelessly to execute her plan. She spread malicious rumors about Isabella in the press, telling reporters that the actress was difcult to work with and had a bad attitude on set. She also began to manipulate key players in Hollywood, convincing directors and producers not to work with Isabella on future projects.

Despite all of this, Isabella remained blissfully unaware of Victoria's scheming. She continued to bask in the success of her career, attending glamorous events and receiving accolades for her performances. However, it wasn't long before Isabella began to feel the effects of

Victoria's jealousy. She noticed that offers for new roles began to dry up, and that directors who had previously been eager to work with her suddenly seemed distant and uninterested.

Isabella was confused and hurt by the sudden change in attitude towards her, but she refused to let Victoria's jealousy get the best of her. She continued to work hard and remain focused on her career, determined to overcome any obstacles that came her way. As time passed, Isabella began to realize that she needed to confront Victoria if she wanted to salvage her career. She knew that Victoria's jealousy was the only thing standing in the way of her continued success, and so she began to plot a plan of her own. One night, at a Hollywood party, Isabella fnally came face to face with Victoria. The two women exchanged icy glares as they stood across from each other, and it was clear that tensions were running high.

But instead of engaging in petty arguments or further confict, Isabella surprised everyone by extending an olive branch to Victoria. She offered to work with her on a new project, hoping that by doing so, she could mend their broken relationship and put an end to the jealous rivalry once and for all.

To everyone's surprise, Victoria accepted Isabella's offer, and the two women began working together on a new movie. It was a large scale production that would require them to work closely together for months on end, but Isabella was determined to make it work. And in the end, Isabella's determination paid off. The movie was a huge success, and both actresses received critical acclaim for their performances. Their rivalry had been replaced with mutual respect and admiration, and Hollywood was abuzz with talk of the two women who had put aside their differences and come together to create something truly special.

As Isabella refected on the events that had transpired over the past few months, she couldn't help but feel grateful for the experience. She had learned that sometimes, even your worst enemies can become your greatest allies, and that success is not always about conquering others but rather about fnding common ground and working together to achieve your goals.

With a newfound sense of confdence and purpose, Isabella continued to rise to new heights in her career, proving to the world that even in the face of adversity, she was a force to be reckoned with.

Pressing Issues.

As Isabella's star continued to rise, she encountered a new set of challenges that threatened to derail her career. Negative press and rumors began to circulate, with Victoria, a rival actress, at the forefront of it all. Isabella was determined to maintain her success and overcome these obstacles, but she couldn't do it alone.

Enter Julia - Isabella's trusted confdante and PR guru. Julia was devoted to Isabella and worked tirelessly to protect her reputation. She knew that Isabella's success was not only important to her client but also to herself. After all, Isabella's stardom was Julia's ticket to living the glamorous life she had always dreamed of.

Together, Isabella and Julia embarked on a mission to combat the negative press. They understood the importance of controlling their narrative and decided to take matters into their own hands. Large-scale events were organized, press junkets were scheduled, interviews were granted - all in an effort to shift the conversation away from the rumors and towards Isabella's undeniable talent.

But Victoria was not one to be outdone. She continued to plot against Isabella, determined to bring her down. The tension between the two actresses was palpable, and the media ate it up. Every move they made was scrutinized, every word they spoke analyzed. As the drama unfolded, Isabella found herself questioning her own worth. Was she really deserving of this level of success? Or was it all just a fuke? But Julia refused to let her client fall into a pit of self-doubt. She reminded Isabella of all the hard work she had put in, all the sacrifces she had made, and all the obstacles she had already overcome.

With Julia by her side, Isabella regained her confdence and pushed forward. She refused to let Victoria win. Even when it seemed like all hope was lost, Isabella remained determined. And slowly but surely, the tides began to turn. The negative press subsided, and Isabella's talent once again took center stage.

Looking back on those tumultuous months, Isabella couldn't help but feel grateful for the experience. Through it all, she had learned that success was not just about talent - it was also about resilience, determination, and a little bit of luck. And with Julia by her side, she knew that she could conquer anything that came her way.

Chapter 12
Fame's Guardian

Isabella felt a sense of awe as she stepped out of the sleek black car that had driven her to the glamorous event. The bright lights of the paparazzi fashed around her, and she could hear the sound of adoring fans screaming her name. Despite the chaos around her, Isabella felt incredibly grateful for everything that had come her way. Her long, black hair shone like ebony in the lights as she made her way down the red carpet, accompanied by her loyal personal assistant, Julia. Julia was focused and vigilant, ensuring that Isabella avoided any negative publicity or scandalous situations. Her short, blonde hair was styled in a sleek bob, and her brown eyes sparkled with determination. Together, Isabella and Julia navigated the chaotic world of fame with grace and poise, their bond as strong as ever. Isabella knew that she could count on Julia to protect her from the pitfalls of fame. As Isabella entered the event, she couldn't help but feel overwhelmed by the large-scale of it all. She had attended countless events like this before, but every time she stepped onto the red carpet, she felt like it was a new experience.

Julia remained close by Isabella's side throughout the night, making sure that she mingled with the right people and avoided anyone who might cause trouble. Isabella was grateful for Julia's guidance and support. She knew that without her personal assistant's watchful eye, she could easily fall victim to Victoria's cruel machinations. Despite Victoria's best efforts to bring Isabella down, she continued to rise in popularity and success. Isabella knew that it wasn't just about talent; it was about resilience, determination, and a little bit of luck. 29

As Isabella accepted awards and accolades throughout the night, she couldn't help but think about the challenges she had faced in her career so far. Negative press and rumors spread by Victoria had threatened to derail her success, but with Julia's help, she had navigated those challenges with poise and grace.

Isabella couldn't deny that the world of fame was a curious one. It was a world that demanded perfection at all times, and even the slightest misstep could spell disaster. But with Julia by her side, Isabella felt confdent that she could weather any storm. As the night wore on, Isabella basked in the glow of her success. She knew that there would be more challenges and obstacles to overcome in the future, but she was ready for them. With Julia watching her back, Isabella knew that she could conquer anything that came her way.

Looking back on those tumultuous months, Isabella couldn't help but feel grateful for the experience. She had learned so much about herself and about the world of fame. And through it all, she had gained a deep appreciation for the power of true friendship.

As the event came to an end and Isabella made her way back to the car, she felt a sense of contentment wash over her. She knew that there would be more events like this in the future, but she was ready for whatever came her way. With Julia by her side, Isabella felt like there was nothing she couldn't accomplish.

Chapter 13
Beyond Acting

Isabella sat in her lavish penthouse, scrolling through her social media feed as she sipped on a glass of red wine. Despite her success as an actress, Isabella had always felt a desire to branch out and explore other areas of the entertainment industry. This was why she recently decided to dip her toes into the world of fashion and philanthropy. As she scrolled through pictures of her latest photoshoot, she couldn't help but feel a sense of contentment. Her career was thriving, and now she had the opportunity to make a difference in other ways. Julia, her efcient and loyal personal assistant, entered the room with a folder full of proposals for Isabella's new ventures. With her short blonde hair neatly styled and her brown eyes focused on the task at hand, Julia presented the options to Isabella, already anticipating her boss's every need.

As Isabella fipped through the proposals, she couldn't help but feel a sense of excitement. She knew that branching out into other areas would be a challenge, but it was one she was ready to take on. The fashion industry had always intrigued her, and now she had the chance to create her own line.

Isabella's mind raced with ideas as she looked at sketches of dresses and accessories. She could see herself wearing them on the red carpet or at events. But there was more to her vision than just clothes. She wanted to use her platform to make a difference in people's lives.

This is where philanthropy came in. Isabella had always been passionate about giving back, and now she had the means to do so on a larger scale. She looked through proposals for various charities and organizations, each with their own mission and impact. As Isabella discussed each proposal with Julia, her excitement grew. She could feel herself becoming more than just an actress; she was becoming a force for change.

The pacing of Isabella's new ventures was well-constructed. Each proposal was carefully considered, and every detail was thought out. Isabella knew that she couldn't take on everything at once, but she was determined to make each venture a success.

As she and Julia worked through the proposals, Isabella couldn't help but think back to the challenges she had faced in her career. The negative press and rumors spread by Victoria had been tough to navigate, but with Julia's help, she had overcome them. Now, with Julia by her side once again, Isabella felt like there was nothing she couldn't accomplish.

Isabella's ventures into fashion and philanthropy were large-scale, but she was ready for the challenge. Her success as an actress had opened doors for her, and now she had the opportunity to make a difference in the world. It was a curious journey she was embarking on, but it was one that she was excited to take.

Chapter 14

Isabella had always known that her foray into fashion and philanthropy would not be a walk in the park. She was entering a world outside of her comfort zone, but one that she was determined to thrive in. Her success as an actress had opened doors for her, but it had also made her the target of critics who doubted her abilities and accused her of being superfcial.

Isabella felt the sting of their words like a physical blow. She was desperate to prove them wrong, to show that she was more than just a pretty face. Her passion for acting was what drove her, and she wanted to be recognized for her talent and hard work.

Julia, Isabella's loyal friend and confdante, was equally determined to protect Isabella's reputation. She took on any challenges that came their way with a ferce determination and unwavering loyalty. She knew that Isabella's success meant everything to her, and she would do anything to ensure it.

Victoria, on the other hand, saw Isabella's vulnerability as an opportunity. She had always been jealous of Isabella's success and desire for fame motivated every move she made. She saw this as a chance to further her own career at the expense of her rival. The criticism from the media was unrelenting. They accused Isabella of being superfcial and using her fame for personal gain. It seemed like no matter what she did, she couldn't shake the negative press. But Isabella refused to let it get to her. She knew that she was more than just a pretty face, and she was determined to prove it. As Isabella threw herself into her philanthropic work, she found

fulfllment in helping others. Her ventures were large-scale, but she relished the challenge. It was a curious journey she was embarking on, but one that excited her at every turn.

Despite the backlash from critics, Isabella continued to pursue her passion for acting. She threw herself into her roles with an intensity that left her exhausted but exhilarated. Her performances were nothing short of breathtaking, and even her harshest critics couldn't deny her talent.

With Julia by her side, Isabella weathered the storm of negative press and emerged stronger than ever. Her determination and hard work were paying off, and she was fnally getting the recognition she deserved.

In the end, the critics could say what they wanted, but Isabella knew the truth. She was more than just a pretty face; she was a force to be reckoned with. And as she continued to conquer new challenges and blaze new trails, she proved it time and time again.

Chapter 15
Persistence Pays Off.

The lights were glaringly bright, casting a warm glow on the faces of the audience that flled the enormous room. Isabella took a deep breath as she stepped onto the stage, feeling the weight of her own expectations for herself bearing down upon her. But she refused to let it show, standing tall and straight-backed, her confdence radiating from every pore.

Julia walked beside her, her sharp eyes scanning the crowd for any potential threats that could derail Isabella's success. Her blonde hair was styled in a sleek bob that framed her face perfectly, and her brown eyes sparkled with an unyielding determination to protect her charge at all costs.

As Isabella began to speak, her words rang out across the large scale room, flling every inch with a power and conviction that could not be ignored. She spoke of her journey from a small town girl to a wildly successful entrepreneur, detailing the struggles and obstacles she had encountered along the way with an air of curiosity that left even her harshest critics captivated.

Despite the success she had achieved, there were still those who doubted her abilities and dismissed her as nothing more than a pretty face. But Isabella remained true to herself, working hard day in and day out to prove them wrong. And as she spoke, it became clear that she was more than just a surface-level celebrity - she was a force to be reckoned with.

The pacing was well-constructed, with Isabella's words building steadily in intensity until they reached a crescendo that left the audience breathless. And through it all, Julia remained by her side, ready to step in at a moment's notice should anything go awry. As the speech came to an end, Isabella basked in the thunderous applause that erupted from the crowd. She knew that there would always be naysayers and critics lurking in the shadows, eager to tear down anyone who dared to reach for the stars. But she refused to let them dim her light, continuing to work hard and remain true to herself, proving them wrong time and time again.

And as she stepped off the stage, a feeling of satisfaction washed over her - she had done it. She had conquered the challenges, navigated the pitfalls of fame, and emerged victorious on the other side. And with Julia by her side, she knew that there was nothing she couldn't achieve.

Chapter 16
Showdown on Stage

The momentous occasion was fnally here, and Isabella could feel the weight of the world on her slender shoulders. Her latest premiere loomed large on the horizon, and with it came a sense of unease that she couldn't quite shake. For weeks now, she had been dogged by rumors and whispers of sabotage, all pointing to one person - Victoria. The very thought of her rival made Isabella's blood boil, but she knew better than to let her emotions get the best of her. She was a professional, after all, and she had worked far too hard to let someone like Victoria derail her career.

As she walked down the red carpet, Isabella could feel the eyes of the world upon her. Cameras fashed, reporters shouted questions, and fans screamed her name. It was all so overwhelming and exhilarating at the same time, and Isabella couldn't help but be swept up in the moment. But then she saw Victoria from across the way, standing there with a wicked grin on her face. Isabella's heart sank, and she knew that this was just the beginning.

Victoria was a force to be reckoned with - there was no denying that. With her striking red hair and piercing blue eyes, she cut an imposing fgure wherever she went. And yet, beneath that cruel exterior lay something even more dangerous - envy. Victoria had always been jealous of Isabella's success, always looking for ways to tear her down and make herself feel better by comparison. Isabella knew this all too well, and it made her skin crawl to think of what Victoria might do next. But for now, Isabella had to focus on the task at hand - navigating the premiere with grace and poise. Julia was by her side as always, offering words of encouragement and a steady hand to hold onto when things got tough. Isabella felt grateful for her friend's unwavering support, even as she felt the weight of her own doubts pressing down upon her.

As she made her way inside, Isabella could hear the murmurs of the crowd growing louder. They were all here to see her, to witness the magic that she had created on screen. But at the same time, they were also here to see if Victoria would make good on her threats of sabotage. Isabella couldn't help but wonder what form that sabotage might take - would Victoria try to trip her on stage? Or perhaps she would plant some damning evidence in her dressing room? The possibilities were endless, and they all flled Isabella with a sense of dread that she couldn't shake.

But then, just as she was about to step out onto the stage, Isabella saw something that made her heart skip a beat. Victoria was standing there in the wings, a look of pure malice on her face. Isabella knew then that this was it - Victoria was going to try and ruin her big night once and for all.

As she took the stage, Isabella could feel the eyes of the world upon her. The lights were bright, the applause thunderous, and yet all she could think about was Victoria lurking in the shadows. It was like a game of cat and mouse, with Victoria always one step ahead of her. For a moment, Isabella's confdence wavered - what if Victoria had already done something to ruin her performance? What if this was it - the end of her career as she knew it?

But then something strange happened. As Isabella began to speak, she could feel herself being lifted up by an unseen force. It was like all of her fears and doubts were being washed away by a wave of pure energy and excitement. This was what she had been working towards all these years - this moment right here. And no matter what Victoria

might do to try and stop her, Isabella knew that she could not be defeated.

And then, just as she was fnishing up her speech, Victoria made her move. She stepped out onto the stage, a look of pure venom in her eyes. Isabella felt a sense of dread wash over her like a cold shower, but she knew that she could not back down. Not now, not ever. And that's when it happened - the confrontation that would go down in history. Victoria lunged at Isabella, screaming insults and accusations in a voice that echoed throughout the auditorium. But Isabella stood her ground, her eyes blazing with a ferce determination that Victoria could never hope to match.

For what seemed like an eternity, the two actresses stood there locked in a battle of wills. It was like watching two titans clash - each one determined to emerge victorious at any cost. And yet, despite all of Victoria's efforts to crush her spirit, Isabella remained unbroken. In the end, it was Isabella who emerged triumphant. She had faced down her greatest enemy and emerged victorious, leaving Victoria to slink away into the shadows with nothing but bitter defeat to show for all of her efforts. And as Isabella stepped off the stage, a feeling of satisfaction washed over her - she had done it. She had conquered the challenges, navigated the pitfalls of fame, and emerged victorious on the other side. And with Julia by her side, she knew that there was nothing she couldn't achieve.

Graceful Confrontation

As the music faded and the curtain drew back, Isabella stepped off the stage to a thunderous applause. She had delivered an electrifying performance, and the audience was chanting her name. She felt a wave of satisfaction wash over her - she had done it. Isabella had conquered the challenges, navigated the pitfalls of fame, and emerged victorious on the other side. And with Julia by her side, she knew that there was nothing she couldn't achieve.

But as she made her way to the dressing room, she could feel a storm brewing. Victoria, her rival and a constant thorn in her side, was waiting for her. The two actresses had been at each other's throats since they began their careers, but Victoria's recent attempts to sabotage Isabella's career had reached new heights. And now, in a public confrontation, she was determined to bring her down once and for all.

The air was charged with tension as Isabella approached Victoria. Her rival stood tall and imposing, her eyes cold and calculating. But Isabella refused to back down. She stood with her head held high, determined to show Victoria that she would not be brought down by her manipulations.

The exchange was heated, with accusations flying back and forth between the two women. But Isabella remained calm and composed, refusing to let Victoria get the best of her. She spoke with eloquence and conviction, defending herself against Victoria's baseless claims with ease.

Victoria tried to break her down with insults and snide remarks, but Isabella held steady. She refused to stoop to Victoria's level and remained focused on protecting her reputation and integrity. Her motivation was clear - how she handled this situation would impact how people perceived her.

As the confrontation drew to a close, a sense of satisfaction washed over Isabella once again. She had handled herself with grace and poise, earning the respect and admiration of her peers. Victoria, on the other hand, was left fuming and defeated. Her envy and desire to see Isabella fail had clouded her judgment, and she had underestimated the strength and determination of her rival.

In the end, Isabella emerged victorious yet again. She had proven that she was more than just a pretty face - that she was a force to be reckoned with. And as she left the theater that night, she knew that she had taken another step towards achieving her dreams.

The confrontation may have been small-scale, but its impact was large-scale. It was a triumph of integrity over manipulation, of grace over pettiness. Isabella had shown that she was a true artist, committed to her craft and unwilling to compromise her values for the sake of success.

As for Victoria, she was forced to confront the reality that her actions had consequences. She had lost the respect of her peers and damaged her own career in the process. But even in defeat, there was a sense of curiosity about her - what would she do next? Would she learn from her mistakes and try to make amends? Or would she continue down the path of envy and destruction?

Only time would tell. But for Isabella, there was no doubt - she was on the rise, and nothing could stop her now.

Chapter 18
Love's Unwavering Strength

Isabella and Marcus sit across from each other at a candlelit table in a cozy Italian restaurant. The ambiance is warm and welcoming, and the smell of freshly cooked food infuses the air with its tantalizing aroma. As they chat, they seem at ease, enjoying each other's company. Isabella's long black hair falls onto her shoulders, framing her piercing green eyes. She reaches for Marcus's hand across the table and squeezes it tightly. Her heart swells with love for him as he gazes at her with deep brown eyes. For Isabella, this moment is large-scale - it represents her achievements so far and the love that has grown between them.

Marcus's lips curl into a soft smile as he returns her affectionate gaze. He's proud of Isabella's strength and resilience, and grateful to have her in his life. As he looks into her eyes, he sees the passion and determination that has pushed her to succeed despite the odds stacked against her. He admires her courage in the face of Victoria's attempts to derail her career, and he has supported her every step of the way. As they sip their wine, Isabella refects on how far she has come. She has faced many obstacles on her journey to become one of the most prominent actresses of her time. But she remains true to herself, continuing to work hard and prove her critics wrong. She remembers Victoria's attempts to sabotage her career which escalated, culminating in a public confrontation between the two actresses. But Isabella handled it all with grace, earning the respect and admiration of her peers.

She realizes that the struggles have deepened their bond and love for each other. They have stood by each other through thick and thin, encouraging each other when times were tough. And as they sit across from each other now, she knows that nothing can stand between them. The pacing of their conversation is well-constructed - as they talk, they reveal their hopes and dreams for the future. Isabella shares her plans to take on more challenging roles, pushing herself to become a better actress. Marcus listens attentively, his eyes sparkling with admiration and love.

As the night draws to a close, Isabella and Marcus leave the restaurant hand in hand. The stars twinkle above them, casting a curious glow over the city. They walk down the street, enjoying each other's company. For Isabella, this moment represents a turning point in her life. She has faced many challenges and overcome them all with grace and determination. And with Marcus by her side, she knows that anything is possible.

Only time will tell what the future holds for them both - but one thing is certain: Isabella is on the rise, and nothing can stop her now.

Chapter 19
Awards and Accolades.

As Isabella stands on stage, the bright lights casting a halo around her, she feels a sense of awe wash over her. The large-scale audience before her is a testament to her hard work and dedication to her craft. She knows that this moment is the culmination of years of perseverance and sacrifce, and she savors it all the more for it. She accepts the award gracefully, her confdence radiating as she thanks those who have supported her along the way. Her long black hair cascades down her back, framing her piercing green eyes as she speaks with sincerity and humility. Julia stands by her side, ever vigilant and efcient in her role as personal assistant.

As Isabella continues to achieve success after success, winning award after award for her outstanding performances, their partnership grows stronger. They are a powerful team, driven by their shared passion for Isabella's career and their unwavering determination to succeed in the competitive world of acting.

All around them swirls a curious energy, as though fate itself is watching their every move. Isabella knows that nothing can stop her now, that she has overcome all the challenges that Victoria had thrown her way. She has risen above it all with grace and determination, earning the respect and admiration of her peers.

And yet, there is still an air of uncertainty about what the future holds. Isabella knows that success can be feeting, that every victory must be earned anew. But with Marcus by her side, she feels invincible. The future beckons, full of possibilities and potentialities that only time will reveal. But for now, Isabella revels in the moment, basking in the glow of her latest victory. The world is hers for the taking, and nothing can hold her back.

Chapter 20
Union of Power

As Isabella and Marcus stand together at the altar, they are surrounded by a large-scale, ornate church that speaks to the grandeur of their love for each other. The stained-glass windows shimmer with the light of the sun, casting a rainbow of colors across the couple as they exchange vows. Isabella's fowing white gown is a symbol of purity and innocence, while Marcus' sleek black tuxedo represents the formality and sophistication that he exudes.

The ceremony proceeds with a curious tone as the audience watches with bated breath as the couple recites their vows. Isabella's voice is soft and sweet as she promises to love and cherish Marcus for all eternity, while Marcus' deep voice rumbles with assurance as he pledges to always be there for Isabella, no matter what. As they exchange rings, a palpable sense of joy and excitement flls the air. Isabella's piercing green eyes are flled with tears of happiness as she gazes into Marcus' warm brown eyes, knowing that they are now married and bound together forevermore. Their love has been tested and tried, but nothing can shake their commitment to each other. As they are pronounced husband and wife, the audience erupts in cheers and applause, recognizing the power couple that stands before them. Isabella and Marcus exit the church arm in arm, a symbol of their unity and solidarity.

The reception is a lavish affair, one that speaks to their refned elegance and glamorous lifestyle. The room is adorned with large-scale foral arrangements that hint at the opulence of their love for each other. The guests marvel at the exquisite decorations, the sumptuous food, and the lively music that flls the air.

But despite all of this, it is Isabella and Marcus who truly steal the show. They dance together in perfect harmony, moving as one across the dance foor. Isabella's natural grace and beauty are matched only by Marcus' charm and sophistication, making them the perfect pair. As the night wears on, the couple is surrounded by family and friends, all of whom are thrilled to see them together. Isabella's success in her career has been hard-won, but she knows that it pales in comparison to the love and commitment that she shares with Marcus. And as they depart the reception, arm in arm, on their way to their honeymoon, Isabella knows that the future is full of possibilities and potentialities that only time will reveal. But for now, she revels in the moment, basking in the glow of her latest victory. The world is hers for the taking, and nothing can hold her back as long as she has Marcus by her side.

Chapter 21

Championing Causes.

Isabella stands confdently in front of a crowd of reporters, her long black hair shimmering in the sunlight. Her piercing green eyes are flled with determination and passion as she speaks about the important causes she is championing. Julia watches from the sidelines, her short blonde hair pinned neatly behind her ears. Her brown eyes are flled with pride as she observes Isabella using her fame and infuence for good. The two women share a knowing glance, their strong bond still evident even in the midst of this busy event.

Isabella's success had brought her great fame and infuence, and now she was using it to champion important causes that were close to her heart. She had become a philanthropist and role model, inspiring others to do good in the world.

As she stood on that stage, Isabella was larger than life. Her presence was imposing, commanding attention from all those present. But it wasn't just her physical stature that made her seem larger than life - it was also her spirit. Isabella was a force to be reckoned with, a woman who refused to back down when faced with injustice. The causes she was championing were large-scale, tackling issues that affected millions of people around the world. But Isabella didn't shy away from the challenge. Instead, she embraced it with open arms, determined to make a difference.

Her voice was clear and steady as she spoke about the importance of education for underprivileged children. Her words were like music to the ears of those who listened, each sentence perfectly crafted to convey her message with clarity and precision.

Julia watched from the sidelines, flled with admiration for her friend. She could see the passion burning in Isabella's eyes, could feel the determination radiating off of her in waves. There was no doubt in Julia's mind that Isabella would change the world one day - and she was honored to stand by her side as she did it.

The reporters jotted down notes, their pens moving quickly across the paper as they tried to capture every word. They knew that Isabella was someone special, someone who could make a real difference in the world.

And as Isabella fnished her speech, the crowd erupted into applause. It was a heartwarming moment, one that flled Isabella with a sense of pride and accomplishment. She knew that she had a long road ahead of her - but with her fame and infuence, she was determined to make the world a better place, one cause at a time.

Chapter 22

Humility Amidst Fame.

Isabella sat in her large-scale dressing room, surrounded by a team of stylists and makeup artists. Despite the luxurious surroundings, she remained grounded, valuing relationships and her personal life above all else. Her piercing green eyes sparkled with warmth as she chatted and joked with her team, showing genuine interest in their lives. It was this authenticity that had endeared her to so many fans and colleagues alike.

As she prepared for another awards ceremony, Isabella couldn't help but refect on the sacrifces that had been made to get to this point. She had worked tirelessly to hone her craft, spending countless hours rehearsing and studying scripts. But it wasn't just her own hard work that had led to her success - she knew that none of it would have been possible without the unwavering support of her loved ones. Her personal assistant Julia watched from the sidelines, observing Isabella's interactions with a proud smile on her face. She had been with Isabella since the beginning of her career and knew better than anyone the struggles they had faced together. But even in the midst of chaos and stress, Isabella had always remained focused on what was truly important.

As the ceremony began, Isabella took to the stage to accept yet another award. The audience erupted into applause as she stepped forward, her black gown shimmering under the bright lights. But as she began to speak, it was clear that this was more than just another acceptance speech.

"My success is not mine alone," she said, her voice ringing out 50 across the auditorium. "It is thanks to the love and support of my family and friends that I am standing here today."

The sincerity in her words was palpable, and the audience listened raptly as she continued.

"But even as I stand here surrounded by accolades and fame, I know that these things are nothing compared to the relationships that I have built throughout my life. They are what truly matter and what make my life worth living."

As she fnished her speech, the crowd erupted into applause once again. It was a heartwarming moment, one that flled Isabella with a sense of pride and accomplishment. She knew that she had a long road ahead of her - but with her fame and infuence, she was determined to make the world a better place, one cause at a time.

And as she stepped off the stage and made her way back to her dressing room, she couldn't help but smile at the thought of all the people who had helped her along the way. From her family and friends to her talented team, they were all part of the reason why she had achieved such great success. She knew that no matter what came next, they would be there for her every step of the way.

And so, as Isabella settled into her chair and began to remove her makeup, it was with a sense of gratitude and contentment that she refected on all that she had accomplished. She was a true star in every sense of the word - but more than anything, she was a symbol of what could be achieved when one remained true to themselves and never lost sight of what truly mattered.

Chapter 23
Everlasting Bond

As Isabella settled into her chair, she couldn't help but feel grateful for the important people in her life. She reached for a tissue and delicately began to remove her makeup, accompanied by the sound of Julia's comforting voice.

The two had been through so much together - from the early days of Isabella's career to the heights of her success. And yet, despite it all, their bond had only grown stronger. Julia had remained a steadfast presence in Isabella's life, offering unwavering support and guidance when she needed it most.

As they chatted and laughed, Isabella couldn't help but feel a sense of calm wash over her. Julia had become more than just a personal assistant - she was a dear friend who knew her better than anyone else. Their friendship was large-scale, spanning years of shared experiences and memories. They had traveled the world together, meeting new people and immersing themselves in new cultures. And through it all, they had remained grounded and true to their values. Isabella valued Julia's loyalty above all else. She knew that no matter what came their way, Julia would always be there for her - a guiding light in times of darkness.

For Julia, being there for Isabella was a privilege that she cherished every day. It was an honor to be part of such an incredible woman's life, to witness firsthand all that she had accomplished and overcome. And yet, despite their different positions in life, they found comfort in each other's company. They laughed at each other's jokes and finished each other's sentences. They were two sides of the same coin - different yet complementary in every way.

As Isabella removed the final traces of makeup from her face, she couldn't help but feel a sense of awe at how far she had come. She had achieved so much in her career, becoming a symbol of hope and inspiration for so many.

But it was her friendships and relationships that truly mattered to her.

With Julia by her side, she felt invincible, ready to take on whatever challenges lay ahead.

As they said their goodbyes and parted ways for the night, Isabella couldn't help but feel a sense of wonder at the incredible journey she had been on. She knew that no matter what came next, Julia would be there for her every step of the way.

And so, as she closed her eyes and drifted off to sleep, Isabella smiled contentedly, knowing that she was blessed to have such a wonderful friend in her life.

Chapter 24
Balancing Act

As Isabella sat in her dressing room, poring over her script, the weight of her responsibilities lay heavily upon her. She was a woman of large scale ambition, determined to make her mark on the world. But as much as she loved her work, she knew that it came at a cost. Her marriage to Marcus had always been one of the most important things in her life, and she couldn't help but worry that their busy schedules were driving them apart.

Marcus, for his part, was equally preoccupied. He stood at the window of their penthouse apartment, looking out over the city below. For a moment, he felt like he was looking down on everything – like he was in control of it all. But then he remembered the things that really mattered: his love for Isabella and their life together.

It was a curious thing, this sense of balance and imbalance that they both felt. The ebb and fow of their lives, as they tried to juggle their careers and their personal relationship, was like a tide that never stopped moving.

Isabella's green eyes darted across the page, searching for clues about the character she was playing. She wondered if there was some kind of symbolism in the story – some larger message about life and love that she could apply to her own situation. But as much as she searched, nothing came to her.

Meanwhile, Marcus tried to think of ways to support his wife. He knew that she was feeling overwhelmed, and he wanted to be there for her. But it wasn't always easy – sometimes it felt like they were ships passing in the night.

The pacing of their lives was relentless. They moved from one project to the next, always pushing themselves harder and farther. But as much as they loved what they did, they knew that they needed each other more than anything else.

It was like trying to balance on a tightrope – one false step could send them tumbling down. But they were determined to make it work – to fnd a way to keep their love alive amidst the chaos of their lives. As

Isabella closed her script and stood up, she knew that there were no easy answers. But she also knew that she was lucky to have Marcus by her side. Together, they would face whatever challenges came their way.

And so, as they walked hand-in-hand out of the theatre, they both felt a sense of gratitude for the life they had built together. It wasn't always easy, but it was worth it – every single day.

Chapter 25
New Life Arrival

Isabella and Marcus had always known that adding a child to their lives would be a large-scale event. It was a new layer of complexity, a new challenge that they were both eager to face together.

As Isabella held their newborn baby in her arms, she felt a sense of wonder and awe at the little life that they had created. Every tiny detail was scrutinized with curious eyes – the way the baby's fngers curled around hers, the soft futtering of eyelashes as he slept, and the sweet sound of his coos.

But even in these moments of blissful joy, Isabella's mind was also focused on her career. She knew that balancing motherhood and acting would be difcult, but she was determined to make it work. Her long black hair was often in a messy bun as she rushed between rehearsals and diaper changes. Marcus, on the other hand, had adjusted easily to fatherhood. He loved doting on their baby and spoiling Isabella with expensive gifts.

His deep brown eyes would light up whenever he held the baby, and he couldn't resist showing off pictures of their family to anyone who would look. Together, they were learning the joys and challenges of parenting as they navigated this new chapter in their lives. As Isabella sat in her dressing room, nursing her baby before her next scene, she cou dn't help but marvel at the miracle of life. The symbolism of creation and growth was not lost on her as she watched her baby grow stronger each day.

But with this new addition to their family came even greater respcnsibility. Isabella felt the weight of motherhood on her shoulders as she juggled her acting career with late-night feedings and soothing cries.

And yet, despite the challenges, she never lost sight of what truly mattered – her relationships and personal life. Her friendship with Julia remained an integral part of her life, and she made sure to prioritize date nights with Marcus whenever they could.

Together, they continued to face whatever challenges came their way. And as they walked hand-in-hand out of the theatre, with their baby nestled in a carrier against Isabella's chest, they both felt a sense of gratitude for the life they had built together.

It wasn't always easy, but it was worth it – every single day.

Chapter 26
Betrayed Ambition

As Isabella and Marcus exited the theatre, hand-in-hand, they couldn't help but feel a sense of euphoria. Not only had they just watched an incredible piece of art, but they had done it with their beloved child nestled close against Isabella's chest.

Despite the constant challenges they faced in balancing their careers, marriage, and personal lives, Isabella remained determined to use her fame and success for good. Her passion for making a positive impact on the world had only grown since becoming a mother. However, one person seemed determined to stand in her way – Victoria. Consumed by jealousy and bitterness towards Isabella's success, Victoria was willing to take increasingly desperate measures to bring her down.

But Isabella was not one to be easily deterred. She remained confident in her abilities to navigate any obstacle thrown her way. She knew that Victoria's tactics were unethical and would ultimately lead to her own downfall.

As Victoria's attempts at sabotage continued, audiences began to turn against her. Industry professionals recognized her behavior as unprofessional and damaging to the industry as a whole. And with each failed attempt, Victoria's resentment towards Isabella only grew stronger.

The tension between the two women reached a large-scale tipping point when Victoria's unethical tactics were exposed to the public. Her reputation crumbled as quickly as it had been built up, leaving her with few allies and even fewer job prospects.

Isabella, on the other hand, remained steadfast in her determination to use her platform for good. She continued to conquer new challenges with grace and poise, never forgetting the tremendous responsibility that came with her success.

As she looked back on the events that had led her to this point – the challenges, the triumphs, and the betrayals – she couldn't help but feel grateful for the life she had built with Marcus and their child. It wasn't always easy, but it was worth it – every single day.

Chapter 27
Iconic Resilience

The spotlight shone brightly on Isabella as she stood on the grand stage, her graceful movements captivating the audience. Her piercing green eyes glimmered with pride and determination, showcasing a resilience that had become emblematic of her iconic status. The great hall was flled to capacity, with people from all walks of life eagerly watching the performance before them. Some were there to witness pure artistry, while others had come to experience the awe inspiring phenomenon that was Isabella. Regardless of their reasons for being there, they were all united in their appreciation of her talent. Julia watched from the wings, her short blonde hair pulled back in a sleek bun as she clutched Isabella's dressing gown in her hands. She couldn't help but feel a wave of emotion washing over her as she saw Isabella's strength and resilience, knowing that she had been there for every step of the journey.

It was a large-scale production, with elaborate costumes and intricate choreography. Yet even amidst the grandeur, it was evident that Isabella was the star of the show. Her movements were precise and elegant, with each step and gesture imbued with meaning. As she danced, memories from her past fooded back. The challenges, the triumphs, and the betrayals – all leading up to this moment. But she remained focused, driven by an unshakeable determination to succeed.

The audience was entranced, held captive by the spellbinding performance unfolding before them. And yet, they were also inspired. For in watching Isabella dance with such poise and grace, they were reminded of the power of resilience and perseverance. It was curious, in a way. How one person could embody so much strength and inspire so many others in the process. But that was just part of what made Isabella an icon – her ability to rise above adversity and emerge stronger was nothing short of remarkable. As the performance drew to a close, Isabella took her fnal bow with humility and gratitude. She knew that her success had come with great responsibility, a fact that she never forgot. But in that moment, she allowed herself a mcment of pride and celebration. Julia rushed to her side, the two women embracing in a moment of shared triumph. For they both knew how far they had come, and how much they had overcome together.

And so, as the curtains closed and the lights dimmed, the audience rose to their feet in a standing ovation. For they had witnessed not just a magnifcent performance, but a testament to the power of resilience and determination. And in doing so, Isabella had solidifed her status as an icon – a true inspiration to all those who watched her dance.

Legendary Journey.

As Isabella held the copy of her newly released biography, she couldn't help but feel overwhelmed with emotion. Her green eyes glistened with tears of joy as she read about her incredible journey to success. She had always been motivated by a deep passion for her craft and a desire to leave a lasting impact on the industry. And now, with her story immortalized in print, she knew that her legacy would live on for years to come.

The book was large-scale, flled with colorful prose and vivid imagery that brought Isabella's story to life. It chronicled her early years as a struggling actress, the obstacles she faced as a woman in a male dominated industry, and the triumphs that ultimately solidifed her status as an icon.

As Isabella fipped through the pages, she couldn't help but refect on how far she had come. She had faced countless setbacks and disappointments along the way, but her resilience and determination had never wavered. And now, as she held this book in her hands, she knew that her journey had been worth it.

Standing by her side was Julia, Isabella's loyal personal assistant with short blonde hair and brown eyes. Julia had been with Isabella every step of the way, always looking out for her best interests and ensuring that she remained grounded throughout the ups and downs of fame.

Together, Isabella and Julia celebrated this momentous occasion. It was a symbol of all they had accomplished together - a testament to the power of hard work and perseverance.

As she read through the pages of her biography, Isabella couldn't help but feel curious. She had always been a private person, guarded about her personal life and hesitant to reveal too much about herself to the public. But now, with her story laid bare for all to see, she wondered what others would think of her.

Would they see her as the glamorous and enigmatic actress that she had always striven to be? Or would they see the struggles and hardships that she had faced along the way, the moments of doubt and fear that had threatened to derail her career?

As she pondered these questions, Isabella couldn't help but feel a sense of pride and accomplishment. She had made it to the top of her industry, defying the odds and carving out a place for herself in a world that had once seemed so hostile and unwelcoming.

And now, with her story told in a way that was both informative and engaging, Isabella knew that her legacy would endure. For she had become more than just an actress - she had become a symbol of hope and inspiration for all those who dared to dream big and pursue their passions with unwavering determination.

Chapter 29
Grateful Refection.

Isabella sat at the large table in her elegant estate, with only her closest confdante, Julia, by her side. In this moment, as the journey of her life came to an end, Isabella's main motivation was to refect on the incredible journey that had brought her to this point. She was grateful for the love and support she had received from Julia throughout her career and was acutely aware of how much she owed to her loyal assistant.

As they sat together, Julia's motivation was simple - to comfort and support Isabella in any way possible. She listened intently as Isabella reminisced about the past and contemplated the uncertain future ahead. These two women remained united, ready to face whatever challenges may come their way.

The journey of Isabella had been a large-scale one, flled with trials and tribulations that would have broken a lesser person. But she had persevered, and in doing so had become an icon of resilience and determination. Her story was a curious one, flled with twists and turns that kept her audience captivated until the very end.

Isabella had made it to the top of her industry, defying the odds and carving out a place for herself in a world that had once seemed so hostile and unwelcoming. But she knew that her success was not hers alone. It was the result of the love and support of those around her - family, friends, and fans - who believed in her even when she didn't believe in herself.

As she looked back on her life, Isabella felt a sense of gratitude wash over her. Gratitude for the opportunities she had been given, for the challenges she had overcome, and for the people who had stood by her side through it all. She felt that her life had been a well-constructed masterpiece, each chapter building upon the last to create a story that would endure long after she was gone.

And now, with her story told in a way that was both informative and engaging, Isabella knew that her legacy would endure. For she had become more than just an actress - she had become a symbol of hope and inspiration for all those who dared to dream big and pursue their passions with unwavering determination.

As the sun began to set on the estate, Isabella and Julia sat together in contented silence. They didn't need words to know what the other was thinking - they had been through too much together for that. Instead, they simply savored the moment, grateful for the love and support that had brought them to this point.

For Isabella, the journey was over. But her legacy would endure, a tale of resilience and determination that would inspire generations to come.

Chapter 30
Legacy of Inspiration

The stage was set for an event of large-scale importance, and Isabella stood tall and proud at its center. Her long black hair cascaded down her back, swaying with each movement she made. Julia stood by her side, short blonde hair framing her face as she watched Isabella with admiration and respect. The two women shared a moment of silent gratitude, understanding the immense impact that Isabella's legacy had on the world.

For Isabella, the journey was over. But as the audience listened intently to her wise words and inspiring stories, it was clear that her legacy would endure. A tale of resilience and determination that would inspire generations to come.

As she spoke, her voice carried with it a sense of conviction and passion that was truly remarkable. Her story was one of hardship and struggle, but also one of incredible triumph and success. She had faced adversity head-on, refusing to let it defeat her, and in doing so had become a true icon.

The audience listened with rapt attention as Isabella recounted the challenges she had faced along the way. The long hours of hard work and dedication, the moments of doubt and fear, the setbacks that threatened to derail her progress.

But through it all, Isabella never lost sight of her goals. She remained focused, determined to succeed no matter what obstacles lay in her path. And now, looking out at the faces before her, she knew that her efforts had not been in vain.

As she fnished speaking, there was a thunderous round of applause. Isabella smiled gratefully at the audience, feeling a sense of accomplishment and fulfllment wash over her.

Julia stood by her side, tears welling up in her eyes as she watched Isabella bask in the glow of their adoration. She knew that this would be a moment she would never forget - a moment that would stay with her forever.

And as they left the stage together, Isabella and Julia both felt a sense of bittersweet joy. They knew that Isabella's journey was coming to an end, but they also felt a sense of hope and excitement for what the future held.

Isabella's legacy would continue to inspire future generations, proving that with hard work and determination, anyone could achieve their dreams. And as the sun set on this incredible chapter of her life, Isabella knew that she had left behind a truly remarkable legacy.

www.ingramcontent.com/pod-product-compliance
Ingram Content Group UK Ltd.
Pitfield, Milton Keynes, MK11 3LW, UK
UKHW021420090226
10591UKWH00023B/222